How We Met

IAN GREGSON was born in Manchester and educated at Oxford and Hull. He has written for the *Los Angeles Times Book Review*, and published poems and reviews in the *London Review of Books*, the *TLS* and *Poetry Review*, amongst others. His critical books are *Contemporary Poetry and Postmodernism*; *The Male Image: Representations of Masculinity in Postwar Poetry* (both published by Macmillan); *Postmodern Literature* (Hodder Arnold, 2004), *Character and Satire in Postwar Fiction* (Continuum, 2006) and *The New Poetry In Wales* (University of Wales Press, 2007). He has lived most of his adult life in North Wales where he teaches in the English department at the university in Bangor.

Also by Ian Gregson

POETRY

Call Centre Love Song (shortlisted for The Forward Prize for Best
First Collection, Salt, 2006)

CRITICISM

Contemporary British Poetry and Postmodernism
(Macmillan, 1996)
The Male Image: Representations of Masculinity in Postwar Poetry
(Macmillan, 1997)
Postmodern Literature (Hodder Arnold, 2004)
Character and Satire in Post War Fiction (Continuum, 2006)
The New Poetry in Wales (University of Wales Press, 2007)

How We Met

IAN GREGSON

For David & Christine with Love from Ian

S
SALT

CAMBRIDGE

PUBLISHED BY SALT PUBLISHING
14a High Street, Fulbourn, Cambridge CB21 5DH United Kingdom

© Ian Gregson 2008

The right of Ian Gregson to be identified as the
author of this work has been asserted by him in accordance
with Section 77 of the Copyright, Designs and Patents Act 1988.

Salt Publishing 2008

Printed by the MPG Books Group in the UK

Typeset in Swift 9.5 / 13

ISBN 978 1 84471 480 3 hardback

Salt Publishing Ltd gratefully acknowledges
the financial assistance of Arts Council England

1 3 5 7 9 8 6 4 2

for Ceri

Contents

Acknowledgements

'Crab Lane from the New Flats' was published in *The Honest Ulsterman* and republished in the *Gregory Awards Anthology*.

Sideways at the War

It could be love

or only a bad cold turning him to water,
                its roots in his throat
tickling and its wet petals opening in his nose,
                or mostly height and rain
now he's risen to the nineteenth floor, these changes—
                love, promotion—
glazed at lunchtime, he looks out on the prospect
                of versions of himself
looking out on windows in a series all reflecting
                wall-sized windows,
wavering buildings standing in the sky,
                translucent walkers
through a glinting labyrinth turning into water—
                it could be love
or only how his rheumy vision wanders out
                into global glass
melding him and here with Sydney and New York,
                Paris and Shanghai.

Sideways at the War

I noticed glancing sideways
    In the corner of my eye
A war was flashing and smoking
    And I'd forgotten why.

The war had turned into a thing
    That made itself at home
And lost itself inside my sight—
    A cup a bed a phone.

I watched it sometimes thinking
    It's supposed to make me safer,
Turned away and it slipped from me
    Like deep into the sofa,

Lodged itself in a crevice
    Mostly keeping shtum,
Was harboured in that darkness,
    A pen a pin a crumb.

Those things get lost together
    And change when they combine,
Once out of mind they differ
    And feel no longer mine.

The thought of war goes missing
    And joins a personal shame
And when I turn to face it
    The face has changed its name.

The sun is glinting on metal
    When the bedroom door's ajar,
And through the cracks in the floorboards
    I can hear an aching bazaar

For foreign bits and pieces
        Are scattered around my home,
They spilt across my carpets
        From the TV and the phone,

A whisper climbs from the plughole,
        The window's on the blink
As souks and mountains shimmer
        In sidestreets of how I think

I'm all at sea then worried
        My house is edged with elsewhere
So who I am when I'm at home
        Is neither here nor there:

But the war slipped from my fingers
        As I walked down the street,
My mind was in demand
        From someone I had to meet,

And the traffic was very noisy
        And a window flashed with screens,
It scattered me all over
        To be inside so many scenes,

For even on that corner
        The worldwide twitched its web,
But the war's allure was fading
        Like a broken celeb.

The Scaremonger

I almost bought it. But that colour of mourning,
fleshly blue—it put me off. His creatures were crowded
behind the glinting glass where you could point at them,
huddled beside their heaped shards of ice with printed labels:
chilly names and points of origin, exotic and mundane.
The jaw had dropped on mine, its eyes had seen so much
they couldn't shut: they stared at the walls which were buff
and plain as the envelope his leaflet hid inside.

He knows so much we don't, he reads the codes we can't
and suffers on our behalf. His wakeful knowledge
wears away at him but his cadaverous glamour
stares from our screens and huddles of the famous
where he's safeguarded by the network and endorsed.
His stores have slipped in almost unseen on the high street.
His agents fly to all the major capitals,
they move through airports briskly with their samples.

The price, he says, is *vigilance*, but when you pay
the change he gives you plants itself in your pocket,
biding its time in the warm dark. You dwell on his logo: eyes
watching a careless back, and how it's carried by his vans
nightly, daily, down arterial roads and city streets
delivering his goods. I had to leave,
then stood below his air-vent breathing his sickness out
among the queasy takeaways and warm exhaust.

Postmodernism, Or,

I lost you in the nineteenth century
and going back was terribly hard:
the tangle of Pollocks too dense
to penetrate, the Rothkos so serene
they stopped my steps and all my striving.
History looked too changed this way around,
unlearning computers, blinding the TVs
after the flames retracted and the planes
unstuck themselves from those high floors.
What decade had enveloped you?
The prospect of reliving modernism
scared me, quickening that Loss—a dead
tree, so painful, when its numbed fingers
tingle, recoiling from the cruel flow renewed.
I swam against the tide from the shallow end
of the gallery into the old depths
past a group, mechanical, of students
copying a flat atrocity,
and women who come and go
talking of phallo- and phallogo-.
I was on a mission now, a quest,
impelling me through epochs like rooms
where light and water flickered and the Cloud
was thinning the further I travelled
so the Presence was pressing through until
it pained me with its heat and glare.

Grey Areas

The web of my novel broke
and wasn't a web any more
but fog thickening.

I took a walk. The road was white
as a margin: lights
levitated from the valley.

Lucy drinks some full-fat milk, but then
it leaves a sticky cloud
in Michael's throat—

the colours of my characters
kept running
one into the other.

The council estate was hidden, but from there
dreams billowed through me like dissolving
walls on a foggy motorway

while baas rebounded
down the wooly corridor.
The road was blank as a mind

with sudden entrances—a black-leather
seated creature with a bright
speeding navel, for example—

all my wishes and fears
went walking and talking
like people blurring into one

and I remembered I was
swallowed by a shadow
pursuing me once, or

slowly enveloped
like the willowherb
invaded from their roots,

their bottom halves all fog—
so fertile
they pale into ghosts.

And then I found a field
humming with the fog's edges:
tufts of wool on barbs
and on the gorse and thistles
grey areas like corners
closing on the flies.

Folie à Deux

The law, when their deductions falter,
call on your psychic powers.
Out of the handkerchief and key
they leave you feelings filter
through you or spread like spores
and change you like their colony.
These pieces of a killer
dropped at his scenes of crime
echo a phrase in you that's not yours,
arouse an odour, a colour,
skew you out of your own time.

You want to sit still in your own life
but in the distant rooms of summer
the killer sweats, digests and thinks
and flickers in you as you drive
and hourly in your work as a plumber
eyeing pipes and drains, their slimes,
your shadow in the worried glaze of sinks.

His stride wrongfoots your stride.
The handkerchief that nestled by his crotch
bobbles like a small loose cloud
above the pavements to his crimes.
It wraps you in its foreign weather
mingling fluids like a fuck
remembered in a semi
opened by the key,
desires you feel together.

His voice is lodged in you and smells of scotch.
It skews you out of your own place
as though your semi shook
with shouts and then the joining wall were
closing in and pushed you to one side
and you were growing smaller
and flattened like a dummy
buried alive in a case.

Squawks and Speech

Only the parrot observes
his body beside the futon where he tumbled.
Hello, she calls, and again *Hello*—
a voice on a cut-off phone—
and *Come Back Peter*,

calls as though to the voices
and music from downstairs of the lonely TV,
or blackbird near the window where words
extend themselves through the wire
under its solo.

She perches on the spread map
on the table, squawks, and waddles into the sea
off Anglesey, her *Come Back Peter*
as though she's searching for where
he might be really.

Her hunger surprises her,
the cold withering of habitat that started
when Peter changed from upright to flat—
a tree in the rainforest
that echoes briefly,

thunders across silent miles
then joins the endless cycle of decay and growth.
But Peter stays the same, as rush hours
pass him by both ways, and buses
circle around him.

Most days the door's beak opens
and emits, not cries, but letters and newspapers
that sprawl in heaps like speech that tumbles
from a mouth onto the ground
unheard and lies there—

echolalia from outside
repeating his name as though trying to recall
Peter, who he is, and how he fits
into the network of roads—
he's a missing piece,

lost in a room like a mind
with a memory that over and over returns,
a phrase that recurs and calls his name
in a tone that's not his own—
a stuck interior

where the clock is sweeping through
a single season though pollen now is mingling
with the dust on its face, and sunlight
edges across Peter's brow.
The year is tilting

and Peter's eyes are open
so the cat returning squints and mews at his lit
irises, while, buffeting the casement,
gusts cry their one syllable
of a cross baby.

Fallen Women #1–7

An ear, a breast, a fluttering leg,
I search for them and make them whole.
I'm also broken like an egg,
Runny, quirky, and I want control.

Like something I can't *quite* remember,
Pieces fly from me but are a clue
Shivering in raw December.
I make a woman with my glue.

When was it women fell apart?
The legs in subways, bums in trees.
I pick them up. My healing art
Makes only smiling amputees.

I'm always missing the single piece
I rummage restlessly to find
In droppings, feathers and torn fleece,
While eyes observe me from the wind.

Last week I watched my hand escape
Through meadows open like a breach.
It might construct a fuller shape
Grasping at things out of my reach.

A Paper Bag

this piece of you slips from your grasp—
grazes its lips on the pavement,

leaps across the empty road
and soars over suburban gardens

a white blown spirit
aspiring to join the birds

inhaling the cold expanses
of its freedom, its escape,

nuzzling the bark and the stark
branches of a winter beech,

stone crevices of an icy wall
tongueless, toothless, probing with its gums

shaping its lips in a kiss
but finding only ivy and flint,

its skin so tender touching
holly, edgy shards and nettles,

out on its own in expanses
sharp with cats' claws and gulls' beaks,

needy and inhaling and lifted
again into the open air

that tries to tear it,
turn it inside out

as it aches around its small hollow,
its hunger, and shapes its lips

mutely, tongueless, shapes its lips
and mimes its unheard words.

Misconceiving

So many reasons why you shouldn't
   pine for her, the new recruit:
the seventeen years between you, and the wife and kids you love;
   the prospect of suspicion, dispute—
      and you couldn't
     tell her, chance a move.

She's foreign to you and attractive as a niche
   Shadowy in bright cloud, a fading arch.

How many nights now you haven't slept
   but thrown your thoughts toward her
over the river, roads, and the towering city centre
   leaping beyond yourself, that border
     where you've been trapped
     and where you invent her—

A sudden alarm, or free fall off the edge
   Into sleep, a falling short and yearning bridge.

Desire like this resembles loss,
   the seventeen years a waste,
the careful repeated investment in home and career
   building a sense of self—all erased,
     not giving a toss,
     just wanting her near—

Traffic flowing the wrong way, a bridge reaching
   Never to touch, sinews taut with stretching.

How stale these Cheshire lanes have grown,
    the trees repeat their sentences,
thoughts left standing on corners start to rot, a decade
    of looking has heaped up from glances
        into fields stuffed with green,
    with all you've done and said.

Vertigo in a long window, aching stretch,
    A fissure that opens on vistas, shining catch.

    Your wife begins a secret grieving
      over what feels worse than loss—
you're missing but you're here, may not, or may be found but changed:
    she lives on a border looking across—
        misconceiving,
     familiar, estranged:

The soft speaking faces caught up in a bubble
    Staring in her eyes, the dead echoes at her table.

    But she created this character,
      her husband, from pieces of him—
looks, a point of view, ignoring how it shifted, was unstable—
    invented herself thinking "I love him",
        spliced him and her,
      seated, at a table—

Till they came unstuck so in the kitchen fragments
    Fly from their faults, conjectured traits and lost figments.

Surface Impressions

Desire was haunting your crisis
And disrupted all you were.
What made you famous was impressions
Though, infesting you with voices—
Hers was one of many invasions:
How must it feel being her?

So much herself, so singular,
Not scattered by fissions
Into sportsmen, rock stars, politicians—
Not flickering, intermittent.
Practicing one day a fresh mutant,
Briefly in the mirror you were her:

The breathy voice and dirty wit,
Feminist scorn, parodic wiggle.
Gorgeous! Hopeless! Two-faced tit!
All your own words caught up in struggle
As mimic and victim concur—
The face and voice, both neither you nor her.

But tied up with your crisis
Was shock at how your jokes would couple
What should be single, breeding crosses
Mingling yourself with things and people
Till you pined for something singular
And pure, and thought it was her.

Famous voices, but also the babble
From suburbs, hobbies, pubs and jobs
Fell on your wincing, obsessive ears.
Off the street you picked up dry pink gobs
And worked them with your tongue into bubbles
Speaking like all the hims and hers

In cityscapes of wanting, hoping—
All the accents in mouths that water
Over mannequins and travel brochures,
Sucking at cigarettes or straws,
Or twisted in orgasmic shopping:
Wanting and wanting, but not her—

The working jaws, the hungry registers.
Phones rang in your mouth, or the echo
Of desires fixed you in their stucco
As a new impression froze
On your lips. Promiscuous characters,
Those words your mouth holds like a purse:
The searching smoke of both tobacco
And speech. The stubbled or lipsticked Ohs.
The thousand voices coupled with hers.

The Brownie Dress
for Liz, Davie And Matt Faggiani

The times I told
the story of the brownie dress:

I told a policeman first,
when we were twenty, as my alibi
for a car I hadn't stolen
because I'd spent the whole evening
in the Ben Brierley with David Faggiani
of 8 Pym Street,
and he was 5ft 7 with very curly hair
and was wearing a brownie dress
and anyway I can't drive
and, sorry, but where's the car
I'm supposed . . .

A brownie dress?
The constable had seized upon this detail.

Yes, I said,
a friend of his was in the brownies,
Faggiani's with a double g.

But in the pub, a brownie dress?

And it was true that uniform
was very different from the constable's,
his buttons big and silver in the streetlight
of that 3 a.m. in 1973.

And every time I told that story
a decade had passed
and every time
the constable looked younger

and I thought of it again
as Liz was saying that your two friends
from work had come, and you mistimed
your greeting, raising your hand
before they reached your room

and later you told them how
each morning you were glad to wake
and find you had another day
and were sure it could be months

but four days later
you couldn't wake, but called out
at intervals and raised your hand

like someone in their sleep
trying to hail a taxi called tomorrow.

Crab Lane From the New Flats

The flat window can contain Crab Lane and more:
its blackened church, its cobbled hill that climbs
to a growing council estate. I see from here
how its boundaries, bounded by the window,
are lost in Manchester. I try to see
why anecdotes will not contain its past—
the punch-drunk boxer muttering
and shadow-punching through the streets;
the leader of the Whitsuntide procession,
retarded, strutting in army boots and bowler;
my grandfather, who dropped a ladder on his toe,
tied a slipper to his foot, and walked to work—
five miles in the snow. Those characters are caught
between before and after as by photographs,
survive in neither. They withdraw to where they live,
the years between wars as Manchester advances,
not knowing how they are to be enclosed.

How We Met

How We Met

JEREMY LAMB AND SIANED SHARK

**Choreographer, ex-dancer,
Jeremy Lamb is 43**
(or thereabouts, looks older to me).
**Most recently he has starred
as a vampire in films and TV:
in** *Moonfang, Thirsty Dark,*
The Living Were Made of Cardboard,
and *Desires of a Necromancer.*
**All this because four years ago
he danced and sang in a video
famously with Sianed Shark**
(nice link or what?)
the singer with *Compulsion to Repeat,*
composer and musician (28).

JEREMY LAMB

. . . but don't you think celebs mislead
you with their stories made up in advance? . . .

I'd heard their single *Vampire Trance*—
oh heal it heal it so it bleed—
not knowing how our rhyming need
would stir me up, how Ned would hurt me,
and our merging like you'd not believe.

Ned's vulgar fire I envied and her youth,
gauntness and her soft full-blooded mouth,
their hit, which hurt me, *Cruel Hot Love.*

I saw her at a fancy dress party
first out of the corner of my eye
when (this is awkward!) I was bent over
trying to revive my then lover
who had fainted.
                I was bone-dry,
creaking on my last legs, forty—
she revived me. This is the muddle
though, we meant, in *Summer Rain*, our song:
hot weeks and dust that must resist
the moistening that must insist,
the stirring to life that makes it long.
She pushed me about like a nude model,
twisted my stiff limbs—confused
me with the vampire she created
filming her sight-bite *Dancing Dead*.

We're touring now—all gigs and speed,
all bumps and blur. Our voices have mated.

I'm so tired and happy, and somewhat bruised.

SIANED SHARK

Mary I call him.
                He'll say it was a joke
him at the party in his black cloak
biting the throat of that ballerina.
Then I thought there'd been a
version of him long ago
looking like him in my video
sucking the life out of my people.
Strange we're such a loving couple,

him then me each other's teacher,
dancing, composing, talking Nietzsche:
special places we can merge in
ordinary people can't imagine,
chords from other planets like a margin
flickers in the corner of their eye,
déjà vu, tasteful, Gemini—
shadowed outside you like a screen ghost.
What's always disturbed me is his taste:
his food, his wine and camp old aristo clothes,
the crossover of our mouths—
he wanted mine, its redness, fulness, shape.
Also I remember a landscape—

turn off the tape, Melissa, turn off the tape . . .

Not the landscape of my people:
hillsides, steep. Wet slate. The chapel.
Now I'm haunted by the memories
not of my own childhood, but his:
places I've never seen like déjà vu,
an old love hurting like new,
hurting with the urge to repeat—
yearning for his broken dancer's feet
bulging biceps thighs and calves
squiggly with veins: what doubles or halves
me till his face is flushed with my youth,
till it opens redly with my mouth.

MARTHA AGNEW AND KEVIN DANTE

Kevin Dante (39)
is founder of *The Spirit's Gym*:
'the healing regime
where fitness and prayer combine'.
The dancing career
of Martha Agnew (28)
was halted for over a year
by anorexia.
Together they wrote *The Health Hymn*,
'a psalm of the Light and the True Weight',
and *Curves Are Sexier*.

MARTHA AGNEW

I was at the top of the tree
where everyone could see me.
How could I dance and be
looming too large just to be me?
I wanted half to shrivel
and lose control by growing so small

I could fly away—lift, swivel
and fly, but lost it in a fall,
breaking like clockwork.
Noone could piece me together
while Jerry was swallowed by his Shark.

I lay down under the weather
like a bird that's lost its spark
and couldn't work.

And I recoiled from ugly Robin Cage
whose love for me had shifted into rage.

But there are Patterns: here they filled a

gap you know? I needed repairing
so They sent a body builder,
shaped a pairing
that struck me against him like a match.
I fell in the street. Sat down, feeling fat.
He lifted me saying *You don't weigh much*
and carried me back to his flat.
I burrowed downwards through his touch
and curled myself up into nothing—
and turned myself over like a new leaf,
his easy pickup, useful, soothing
as a doll that comes to life,
knowing fame had made me man-nish.
Kevin's a saint. We can diminish

ourselves and shade into a margin
meekly, mildly, that we merge in.
That man pumped up, I imagine—
once I saw him, during a Cure
hover slightly above the floor,
and he can change, at will, my figure—
growing lighter by growing bigger.

So I smile to think one day of Kevin,
feeling a Change not steroids but like leaven
ballooning heavily into heaven.

KEVIN DANTE

When she was coming back from being ill
she twisted her ankle and fell.

It's shocking, the power of her will—
although she plays the underdog.

We crossed so often on our jog,
her ticking over like with anger.
I watched her burning with hunger
flustered and all aslant,
taken by what she must want.

That day was cloudy but the sky
opened, where she fell, one eye,
like a ladder led from the sun—
the time was quick with time, like soon
and once and after all in one.

I touch, and Something intercedes.
The hands on Matha's clock unfroze.
A store sang *heal it till it bleeds.*
A mystery altered our clothes
we stumbled through in search of leads,
straps and supports and springy shoes,
networks of sweat, our rhyming creeds—
baggy tracksuits alive with clues.

But Jeremy Lamb, that camp liar
had written himself all over her skin—
everywhere I could feel where he'd been:
Jerry, who hides that he's a vampire
by hamming it like a role.

He won their struggle for control,
taught her to fly and set her on fire.

And I was left to make her whole
and clear the traces of his message
and the stigmas of her hurting role
with herbs, aromas, weights and massage:

Scapegoat, burning bird and dancing doll,
Jerry shaped her in his vice
until she thought she was that girl
Winter wants as a sacrifice
and dances till her body gives,
dances herself into the ground
till all of Nature lives.

And she fell in love with her own wound.

JAG LEPPARD AND ROBIN CAGE

**Publicity agent
Jag Leppard rose to fame
because Jane Crook attacked him by name
in Parliament,
abusing, some said, her 'privilege'.
His motto is *The Truth Varies*.
Sianed Shark and Robin Cage,
the escapologist,
have gained from the deft twist
he's given their stories.**

JAG LEPPARD

I want to see the text of what I say
before it goes to print OK? . . .

You know this: times your self-image
fogs, the contrast flattens,
colour drains from your screen?
They saved my sanity, did Cage
and Dante who showed me Patterns
composing the picture unseen—
Kevin's a saint, or health sage
and healed me till I knew my needs
were not my wants,
                              but Robin's dwarf
height and thick specs are camouflage
his will so far exceeds
his bounds of body, casts his slough
of self—he's . . . well, a sort of mage.
And days had been too much the same with me
and then the same. He makes things differ
from what they are and as my model
healed me with his manly alchemy:
the wet same days grew sharper, stiffer,
straightening their damp muddle . . .

Words can wriggle free—
manly is not the one you want,
Melissa, there.
                        I teach my clients
words, handcuffed, straitjacketed,

still sidle and slither into print
and shape them with that violence

where lives get marketed—
but Robin evades every curb:

no one believes he was at
the party where we met;
he brims with himself like a verb
and *is* all at once and then he's not,
all out of reach of regret.

He argued with Ms. Shark, that hard babe,
shouted *Fuck it's finished*—
and I loved his dismissive flair
so much—then climbed into a wardrobe,
bellowed some curses and vanished,
flickering in the mirror on its door.

ROBIN CAGE

He said that? Well with Jag it was a struggle . . .

The key, Melissa, is to change
and break and enter and burgle
the beings of others and grow strange—
down to each thinking click and gurgle
even to yourself and change your shape,
your only habit to escape.
But Jag got stuck
with Sianed fixed in his sight
himself all pointed at a fuck,
his string drawn back endlessly tight.
I saw him at Compulsion first,
the band, staring like he was stuck fast.

We talked. He felt ignored
like a tap running till he poured
out of himself in search of her:
Sianed the siren, Jag the temptee
till he blanked his character,
leaking till he was empty . . .
That's the fourth, Melissa, no wonder . . .
No. Whoever looks at you must know this . . .

Well I took him home and put him under,
started to heal him with hypnosis
(as I could for you, for your nicotine,
your nails, your eating,—could remedy them).

Thing is, Jag's refashioned what I've been
to TV, the papers, he's my medium,
changed what I am into a role
to show the public what it can mean
to change and escape. He took control
and I flourished in his image . . .

No, it's true—what Sianed stole,
I wanted to repair that damage,
how he walked like a lost soul
inside his grey suit . . . I was his mage
only in restoring him, his inner—

but meet me at *The Blank Page*
at nine, if you like, and we'll have dinner.

JANE CROOK AND GRACE ROSE

'The male desire for victims haunts
this vilifying of Grace Rose,
the slanders, the jokes and the taunts.
How sadly her case shows
that male frustration vaunts
itself as moral rage.' —
The junior minister
Jane Crook is 44.
She's battled (in this sort of prose)
for over a year
to clear the name of the star
of soap and stage
(who lies about her age).

JANE CROOK

One of the media's versions of her
shocked me: that she was a sick mimic —
phones you as your dead mother, lost lover ...

not the others: handcuffs, pills, bulimic ...
bull dyke ... that famous chef, her recent ex
who claimed she gobbled pork out of his wok,
tied him up with his own socks,
chucked up over his cock
and force-fed him fried pork and sex.

The empty eyes of the whole culture
spread her out above us
while our hungers like a vulture
picked at her body between our covers.

[37]

When I saw her for the first time live
she swooped and soared above the stage . . .

Peter Pan . . . all that demand to believe . . .

and just in front, with this strange look, Robin Cage . . .
sorry, I was struck—my daughter who's five
gasped as she flew. We went backstage
and met this frightened little girl, this Grace
bewildered as though each hostile image
flickered like sun and cloud across her face
until she settled like a screen—

and then her shoulders tightened, she deepened
her voice, and I was watching all I've been
in TV interviews (slightly cheapened)
earnestly explaining what I mean.
She told me—as myself—what it was like
to be confused with images of her
as though her fantasies could leak
and make her guilty as her own voyeur.
Twelve million pricks with Grace in their sight
perked up and pointed, which aroused my anger

that what's desired gets hurt by spite,
and how we're changed in the eyes of a stranger.
Her frailty made me stronger:
I wanted to hold the boy in flight
as though my arms had caught a

briefly pure thing, the way a valley holds mist
or arms of land the dippy water

that can half accept them, and half resist.

GRACE ROSE

There's somebody sometimes
I've no antibodies for,
who maybe who they are rhymes
with something I've lost they could restore,
who then I need to follow, to know
who they are where I can't go.

Jane says it's like I'm on a tour
of where they feel themselves being
most personally, and go there sight-seeing.
Otherwise I'm stuck inside this frame
of who I am and who I am,
the picture's fixed the same and then the same.

When I project I'm freeing
myself, I'm someone at the moment when she's full
of herself like a shy boy
knowing now, YES, this is going to be,
will happen now, this gorgeous pull;
a singer watching massed bodies obey
the moves her tongue shapes and her breath,

or Martha Agnew, such control
of her blazing body it's like growth or death
or both—it tightened round me hard, that role.
I spoke and walked a year in character
and sprouted stigmata hurting like her:
bruising from Jerry, cuts she made that bled

from my arms, their veined soft turn, and my stomach.
Then I mutated like a virus and spread
across the papers like an epidemic.
Guilt, Meliss. I wanted to be punished.

Guilt. You think I'm good? I wanted to see
my image distorted and diminished,

but I got this phonecall from my MP
making a mission out of me—
Jane all furious about men and why.
I sent her a ticket to see me fly
and felt myself give toward her
for her earnest wishing to protect.
I'd curled up tight and lived in purdah,
sick of those fantasies, and worried I infect
innocent others.
                And my eating disorder,
or Martha's? . . . someone else inside you slims
and slims and says you're still not thin . . .

but Jane's a bridge where the sun brims
in your face, and the colours and shapes begin
to begin . . . a hundred happy whims

of shopping and cooking
and standing still and just looking
at tall buildings cars and the flickering sky
where time opens on surprised leisure . . .
daily things she taught me change your stale I

with ordinary pleasure, just pleasure.

JO TOOGOOD AND SIMON LAMB

Jo Toogood's weekly column
Power of Speech
exposes hype and spin

(except her own, the two-faced bitch).
The therapist Simon Lamb
is brother of Jeremy,
the dancer and pop star.
He helps his patients deal with fame—
'delusions of celebrity'
and 'gaps between the self they are
and who they are perceived to be'.

JO TOOGOOD

What shouldn't, Melissa . . .—its power:
turnings away gripped by a flush,
tryings so it won't appear
which DOES, and happens, then is hush hush.

I knew, before, the main stuff—
the phone-call Grace had made to Robin Cage,
half-guessing why it was enough
to start it all, his vengeful rage . . .

and finding myself half in love
just muddled me up with all those names,
with Jeremy, Sianed, Martha and Jag.
I played with Si, at first, games
where yes wavers, and then a snag
because he wanted to be hurt—
it's what he does, absorb the hurt
of everybody to convert
and thrive on, and infuriate
me with his stillness, how he gapes
open gulping it all in

but when he made me free associate
linking the facts and leaping the gaps

I saw a dancer scarred and falling

from ever so high . . .
                        saw a healer levitate
and look as though he knew the answer . . .

saw the dwarf master of escapes
whisper in his agent's ear a luscious lie . . .

a broad man watching from a margin
with blood on his chin . . .

an actress who learned to fly
and turned into a dancer . . .

millions of mirrors with her image in—

the press, TV, oh Grace, the travesty.

I felt empowered. Just to know
all that plot was conquering vertigo
and standing firm above the dizziness
till every wet no hardens into yes.
And know each character, and their address

and watch the gradual light open each street
and alley, and the answers lie at my feet.

SIMON LAMB

'A needy obsession with *healing*'
(Jo wrote) 'is gripping the culture'

but came to me following the spoor
of Robin and what I was concealing
about my brother and Grace and Martha.

She shrank me with her looks like my mother
who always favoured my brother
and told me what I should be feeling.
Jo in my room and the others grow and grow
but change in their versions of each other.
I shrink and back off like a creature
who watches, curled up, from the ceiling

this spectacle of self, of character
like features packed tight into a box,
bound hard between their scalp and their socks
like tightly plotted books.
There's more in me of what I'm not,
no patterns, just the runny blot

and Jo and the others leave a thick growth
of words on my floor I climb through like a sloth
or shrink into like camouflage.

I tire of Jo and her lost plot,
searching the victim and the tyrant
and the sucking of blood out of Grace,
her bearing the sick collective brunt.

She hated you that night in The Blank Page
glancing over the head of Robin Cage,

me glancing back at your clever face
Melissa . . .
                        But your smiles are all a front.

You're all the same. Your drive for power. Your lies—
however much my need complies
with all you victimisers want
to make myself the sacrifice
and solve myself like a long haemorrhage . . .

The William Ewart Gladstone Comic Strip

PART ONE : THE MEDIUM

The Medium : Caricature

1) ATTEMPTING A LIKENESS

Under the pondering detective's eye
The outline of the chalked victim on the floor
Rises and walks backwards from her fate
Into conjectured feeling and flesh.
But reconstructions lack a vital part:
Detective, like cartoonist, travesties
The full-blooded, open-eyed aliveness
Moment by moment of the victim.
Pensive, he doodles her silhouette;
Cross-hatched or limned, she is still life,
Though animated, she can hardly breathe.
Such sketches are premised on a distance
That generalises and belittles
As sun-warmed lovers, splashing and laughing, get
Reduced, a mile away across the beach,
To eight dark limbs and two dark torsos,
And a sketchy scamper like a dog.
The whole of someone else's being
Won't be grasped, but how the victim
Narrowed her eyes enlivens her silhouette—
It's otherwise so close to nothing
Rain falls through it, wind blows it out of shape.

II) Finding Likeness in Unlikeness

The victim smiles from her photograph
But didn't look this way to her husband,
As Feiffer knew who drew a desperado
Loneliness created, plotting to murder
The telephone, his wife's true love.
What never could've happened
Can summon up what did in summary
Execution. So a dream might help me at the start—
Calm General Gordon's cockpit bucks and dives,
His dials whirr, and he ignores the politic
Control tower, where Gladstone tries to talk him down,
But watches the green of England whiten
With adoring upturned faces, and in vain
Pulls his wheel and races down to earth.

III) Exploding Likeness Through Rebellion

For thirty years I published my cartoons
In right-wing dailies: in the floor of print
They opened up a crack revealing
Lower stories, flammable rubbish, oubliettes.
My anger stripped complacent fat
And turned oppressors into victims: fought,
As Grosz did, fire with fire—the tall building in
His *Homage to Oscar Panizza*
Has window frames as stark as a grille—
All Hell is burning behind them;
Or they're like a woodfire's tortured
Skeleton, when, seconds-long,
A gust blows off its living surface.

Or maybe I gave comfort to my enemies.

The Medium: Comic Strip

Since my commission demands
A history-can-be-fun
William Ewart Gladstone Comic Strip,
I've had to multiply the frames:
Motion in fragments, and *fumetti*—
Those balloons for speech and thought.
Each frame's a momentary stay,
Bounding a cleared place
In which an action gets explained.
This ought to reassure, except that,
Flipping through the strips,
All those boundaries so quickly
Flickering by, upset my eyes
With what they can't digest—
Like the *moiré* effect of railings
Rippling across my windscreen
With waves behind them, crosscurrents
And what I can only guess at underneath.

The Medium: Searching for Shape

Sometimes the strips worry
how they only grow, extend—
they want to tell a single story
with beginning, middle and end

but falter . . .

They want to piece the past's
body together bone
by bone, and flesh its ghosts,
each frame a stepping stone—

but water . . .

and each strip is . . .

Worry how the gap is
wide—the next stones disappear—
the water deep—each step is
stalled with longing like a pier

and broken like ellipsis . . .

Part Two: The Strips

My First Victim

Uncle Jim was not my uncle
And he sat in my daddy's chair.
I can't believe my mother picked him.
With his gut and his carbuncle,
Stop mithering and Don't stare,
Uncle Jim was my first victim.

For I knew my real daddy was real,
But Jim had nicked him in one swallow,
Or wore him like a bad disguise.
A hole had opened in all I could feel:
Inside my dad's coat this dad was hollow,
Though my dad looked out through his eyes.

Across the Thirties great waves pressed—
The waves that run across money and land,
Half-human waves that crash and boom—
And carried Jim in his boots and vest,
Pushed him through the bowels of money, and
Voided him in our living-room.

Or Jim had marched across the land
Searching for fruitful living room,
A place where he could be in charge
And let his gut and dick expand:
A kitchen and impressionable womb
Which he could rule by being large.

Some childish premise that expects
Power to be rational and just
Recoils from the crushing weight
Of its damp haunches and connects

The thrust for more with greed and lust—
Sleek cheeks that chew on the State.

So Jim became my prototype
For power and all its alien works:
The whirling wheels and cogs and teeth
Or cunning intestines, quaking tripe,
The monster machine that lurks
Flagrantly inside, beneath.

Too flagrantly. For politics
Is not a body with its drives,
And power's diffuse or unaware:
Its corridors grow blind, unfix
Themselves, are tangled in our lives
But step out abruptly high in the air

Or run down muttering into the ground.
For power slips between the hard lines
Cartoonists draw, evades the frame
Where physical obsessions confound
Personal and political designs,
Pull down the pants of public shame—

Simplistic gesture of rebellion.
Anger at Jim squeezes my eyes,
The simple static fact of greed.
But when I switch the telly on
Power flickers, all its shapes are half-lies,
Shifting, dissolving, like the blur of speed.

The Elastic Band

England became an elastic band,
stretched itself further and further
over raw mountains and whelming sand,
heathen terrain and primitive weather,

frayed its elastic on craggy peaks,
snagged it on jungles, soaked it in seas,
hacked at by Afghans, hacked at by Sikhs—
always and everywhere, new enemies:

These few, these happy few, this band of brothers,
this band could play *God Save the Queen*,
taught the tune to exotic races
but heard in their own thoughts those others
mix a strain of English which would mean
the elastic snapped back in our faces.

Young Dog, Young Cat

The young dog Gladstone
Wears a shiny-bright dog-collar
But it looks as though
His fallen halo's tightened at his neck;
His brow is broad and noble, but
Subverted by his flexing nose —
A connoisseur of dubious breezes,
He tests them, tests them in his vast nostrils . . .
The young cat Disraeli clings
To the greasy pole; his claws slip,
He clings . . . then tries again,
Losing some claws on the climb.
He's gracile but ferocious,
Domestic but exotic.
Husbands beside snoring wives
Half-envy his bright nights
Conjectured beyond their bedrooms,
Envy, too, the risky days —
Trap him in a corner
He'll houdini out,
Pin him down, he'll vanish
Limb by limb, leave only
A translucent smile.

A Beast Fable

Disquiet at one edge of the frame, and then

This blind tunnelling beastling emerges
From a dimlit turn in a winding sentence,
From a devious alley under plausible ground.

Gladstone stumbles on it in the small hours
In his kitchen. It reminds him of dark
Doodles in illuminated books
Infringing from a margin on a reading eye;
Gargoyles leaning into conversations;
Carved horrors under his seat at prayer.

He met it first when, as a boy, following
A fairy tale, he missed the point and found
The wrong path.

               It's like a buried memory
Surfacing through a hole in the nursery floor
But scattering by chairs and tables

Tumps of dust and must from tenements,
Of papers, books and keys from counting-houses,
Secrets from pockets, chests and strong rooms.

So as he looks into the deep
Recesses in its head, its tunnel vision,
He sees the secrets he suspected there—
Which reassures him.

                  But then he glimpses

Tunnels branching from the near tunnel,
Shadows of worries and secrets not familiar
But further concealed and still unworried.

An Enchanted, Perverted, Topsy-Turvy World

'We have much studied and much perfected, of late, the great civilised
invention of the division of labour; only we give it a false name. It is not,
truly speaking, the labour that is divided; but the men:- broken into small
fragments and crumbs of life; so that all the little piece of intelligence that
is left in a man is not enough to make a pin, or a nail, but exhausts itself in
making the point of a pin or a nail.'

— RUSKIN

'It is an enchanted, perverted, topsy-turvy world in which Monsieur le
Capital and Madame la Terre do their ghost-walking as social characters
and at the same time directly as things.'

— MARX

As Ruskin sketched his still life *Sloes*
Anatomising stem and leaf,
A creature scurried across the ground —

An old hand like a detail
Extracted from a master,
A life-like hand and moving
Like a spider on its finger-tips.

It was a calloused factory-hand —
A man or woman much reduced.
For what a piece of work was Man!
A piece-worker now, a work in pieces.

So I've dismantled a working-man,
My frames like mirror fragments;
Jagged edges holding here
A narrowed eye, a tensed elbow; there
A flexed knee, a turning wrist.

But when these pieces assemble,
People are cannibalised in things:
Since men have mated with matter
The misbegotten are on every hand.

Chimeras, monsters of desire:

A balustrade of knobbly knees
A spoon that hides a gargoyle in its face

A chest of drawers

An arm-like pier whose reach exceeds its grasp
A shelf of swells with one akimbo arm

A chest of drawers that's banged up tight

The thick black thought of the smokestacks
Hardening on churches and town halls

A woman with a floral cover, hand-sewn,
Suspension and curled hair in her seat,
Who reaches out, with sharp desire,
Upholstered and enfolding arms.

Brother and Sister

'Sequestered once more as her father's companion, Helen lapsed into
depression and hysteria. The doctors prescribed laudanum and alcohol as
tranquillisers. She was soon addicted . . . Probably Gladstone was only too
aware of how near he himself could come to the kind of breakdown which
overwhelmed his sister. All his life he had been aware of powerful and
intense passions being restrained only by a rigidly systematic self-control.'
— RICHARD SHANNON, Gladstone

This strip is only two frames wide
And oddly one-sided.
Light shines into the right,
On William: only his shadow falls
On Helen, in the left.
The two frames are windows running,
Adjacent, down a tall building.
The left's an ante-room of history
Where Helen listens at the wall—
For in the right there's Church and State
And William's mind aloft
Soaring over his winged collar;
The left's a woman's place
But topsy-turvy—deranged
Furniture, and food
Meeting on plates like a mad
Association of ideas.
Also the left opens
On the claustrophobic expanses
Of a laudanum dream:
A staircase, then another
Winding higher into the dark.
She glances up and sees herself again
Five staircases higher
Gazing down into an abyss.

Romance. Hysteria. Opium.
Yet the passions that consume Helen

Only stoke William up,
Driving him on.
He pushes back, intrepid,
The frontiers of the dark left,
Bringing light from the right.

So it's odd that the right
Weakens now, and William's thoughts
Bubble up in the left;

That light, behind his back,
Has circled round and shines
Redly from the left;

That right and left converge
And form a stereoscope—
Together the two embody
Fully-rounded figures,

And when Helen is on top
Of the staircase looking down
She sees a collar beating its frail
Wings above the abyss.

Re-Animator

After the past's re-animation
Collages blood and nerve and gland,
It's back with a hitching motion
Touching the present with the cold hand,
For instance, of Gladstone's mission,
Pacifying Ireland.

But the past is a body dismembered
Or series of stills with serious gaps
So heavily encumbered
With wishes and fears and perhaps
Its figures look half-timbered
And their animation stops.

For history stitches
Bodies together with parts
Of speech, the way my pencil cross-hatches
A past my present distorts,
A hybrid time whose lost arm itches,
Hybrid longing that reverts,

Searching the present for the past
To heal the gulf between,
Missing a remembered breast
Or piece of ass, to dwell on gaps that mean
We can survive in pieces by moving fast,
Pulling ourselves together scene by scene.

Rescue Work

He sails the good ship *Rescue*
for London is a tossing sea
where girls are bobbing.

The yonder is wild and blue:
although I know he wasn't me
hearing those calls, that sobbing,

I know his pent-up torrents
ached, bewildered his mission,
as though a fear and a wish

rocked his ship with cross-currents,
all my frames with double-vision.
He can hear her: half a fish,

and half a lady, she calls in the night
where paving, tarmac, brick dissolve
into these tides that waver

because he's stirred up by her plight,
swollen, straining at his hard shut valves.
His need is just to save her,

haul her up from where she's sinking—
he'll reform her once he's caught her.
Except this tantalising yonder

melts into marsh unstable and stinking
between the states of land and water
where the mud might suck him under.

An Unlikeness

My mind's been changed by this commission,
Old though I am. This is a strange position
To think of my hero in: lifting
Myself out of and away and drifting
From the girl, the car, estranged from passion,

Into darkest England and Gladstone's mission—
Saving prostitutes. She lifts my stiff hips
Deftly away—for in her fingertips
There's better knowledge than in all
Of Gladstone's conscience. She is supple and small,

Quiet now and slow, but understood the need
That drove us in the backseat with such speed.
But he was driven by obsession—
Missionary, in all except position,
To that backstreet Africa of the soul.

Once I thought he must've, merely to console,
Touched a shoulder, to encourage, squeezed a knee,
And that his hand must've held that memory
Holding his knife amidst his family
Polished and glinting as they eat and chattered.

Caricature suggests we've shattered
Our own image and our pieces have scattered:
Severed arm, evacuated longing,
Spilt content no longer belonging,
Walking finger, footloose leg—all diverge.

Gladstone I thought was severed by an urge
From his own hand: it cabinet it sketched
Monsters of desire—limned, dislimned and cross-hatched,
Begotten not by fusion but by fission,
By the contradictions of his mission.

Zips and buttons! Now we've pulled ourselves apart,
We pull ourselves together—young thing, old fart.
In draughty corners where the self shivers—
Waste ground, parked cars, brief rooms—spent slivers
Of me quiver and live; desire severs

Me from my brief selves; regrets dismember
What I was and wish and can't remember:
Pieces torn from me like scraps of girls borne
On the wind, the tits and bums of Fern and Dawn
Tortured by hawthorne or drowning in puddles.

But my searching for a likeness muddles
Me and Gladstone: continent he coasted kerbs
Content with nouns like Duty, and no verbs.
His actions and words said only what he meant,
Aloof and stiffened like a monument.

An Ill Wind

A vast nose and a turning weathercock—
Inside the nose, a rare easterly
Had turned the city back to front.
Most days the ruling ideas are borne
By westerlies to the hidden poor:
That day their poor breath fogged the wealthy streets,
Microbes with the faces of crossing-sweepers
Swarmed in drawers through lavender and rose-leaves.

The smell then entered Parliament
Representing water and air:
The Commons whitened with handkerchiefs
As though the old windbag made it weep.
Upset, the belly politic
Rumbled in the Thames, and then
The bubbles spoke in the House.

Dr. Morph and Mr. Darwin

Is it a man is it a bird?
A slug a snake a swift? Oh no:
still trailing his Darwin beard

my Morph's a blighted superhero,
longing to stay, one day, the same,
hopping in the dark of a burrow

then a curlew calling its own name,
his lips erupting in a long curved beak,
and then, just crawled out on a harsh shore,

oh no, a sickly hybrid, weak freak,
caught between two beings, all unsure,
watched by a big sky, a stormy cape.

And Darwin regrets: he never meant
his alter ego to escape,
crippled from his botched experiment.

I limn and dislimn, my cross-hatched
animations flicker like fractals.
Morph awakes this time in a scorched

canyon steaming with pterodactyls.
Now he shrivels and grows stiff,
drowning in air through his wracked gills,

cast out as an arthropod,
stuck in the face of a cliff
like a doodle by God.

Dr. Morph and Mr. Gladstone

His silhouette flickered out of line,
Would not conform, then tugged its toes from his,
Was off to live a severed life
In corners, darkening doors.

Morph flickered in Gladstone's drawing-room:
A shadowplay of life-forms
Hatching on his wall, of limned
Creatures and dislimned, of cross-hatched
Animations feuding as soon as they stir . . .

But shadows crowd round Gladstone
Walking the streets of Soho—
Shadows in frock-coats, shadows in skirts,
Limned, dislimned,
The gaslight racking their shapes.

Traffic Island

Impossible, but hot and graphic,
a desert island in the traffic.

To turn a thought into a place
it's bounded as his personal space.

Around him it's all to and fro:
the bearded man's got nowhere to go.

His beard has reached his ragged knee.
It means—the island—what it means to be.

Victorians felt that starting when
so much became beyond our ken.

Beyond our ken was just a notion,
our island's threatened by an ocean.

The soul, its wherefore why and what
is all dissolved in the cannibal's pot.

No point in dwelling on what's inner,
the natives want you for their dinner.

And so I took this old cartoon,
the man alone with his thought balloon.

Since he's alone no matter where
the island's in a city square.

Expanses stare him in the face:
an ocean cramps each person's space.

Mid-Century Calm

A stone names the building '1860'.
Stripping its facade reveals
A roomy framework for my strip.

The coverings on the middle storey,
Though, will not be stripped away:
The curtains, cushions, gilded tapestry,
The lady lost in crinoline,
Allegory in a fretted frame.

But in the attic is a primate
Growing frightened of himself,
His cassock shrinking from the fur
Sprouting on his hands and feet.

And in the basement of the year
The voices of the ragged are condensed
And silenced in the icy enclosure:
Whitefumetti from their breath
Steam to their ceiling and disperse.

I pull back slowly from the house
Letting its facade heal up around it,
And I can hear the noises start—
Polite rock music and internal combustion:
The street-scene looks quite realistic.

Napoleon's Double

'[In Napoleon III] The French ... have not only a caricature of the old Napoleon, they have the old Napoleon himself, caricatured as he must appear in the middle of the nineteenth century.'

— MARX

His father swarmed with repetitions,
Billions of little Boeys in his blood.
His mother's womb had nightmares—
Loaded with blanks she delivered
Only a genetic message:
Kevenhuller, coatee, jackboots.

Oh this engine tradenamed Bonaparte,
This whirring replica
Of cogs and ratchets: new, improved—
Press the button and he conquers Europe.

Hero for the new times, the century
Middle-aged and plump and rich;
Napoleon in a counting-house:
In court he strips to show his vest marked 'N'
And no one notices he's naked.
But my Benday spots, ironic,
Thicken like night and Russian snow
Falling together.

Tadpoles quicken now in the gene pool,
Surface as human in delivery rooms:

Become Napoleon the car-park attendant,
Napoleon the head of Human Resources,
Napoleon pitching Minimum Death Benefit,
Flashing Napoleon in the fast lane,
Napoleon on an 18 handicap—

Piss-proud Napoleon, all his little boneys
Pushing up against a bulging fly.

I Don't Think

There's a need in nature
Now and then, a hunger
In a stretch of country,
In Flanders or near Austerlitz:
Innocent patches, tussocky
Cow pasture; young plateaux
Cut by canyons; wooded valleys
Loud with water and birds—
Hunger for human flesh.
In 1854 were shipped to Turkey
French cockerels, British bulls:
By 1856 there sat the half-
Eaten everywhere on city streets.
But if you'd looked at Inkerman
Then, that also had been eaten,
Limbless trees and chewed turf—
So whose was the hunger?

Victoria Grieving for Albert

The owl Victoria
Is hardly ever seen,
But she is heard
Haunting graveyards
Wooing the dark.
Her head swivels around
Full circle
Peering after the lost one
Behind her, lost behind.
Her moonlight shadow
Crosses the country,
Touching the people
With its cold fingers.

Dummies

I almost could identify
with Browning, how his I

through being worn
by big ideas, gets torn

or alters like many a
form imagined through millenia

quickening selves
until his I dissolves

and someone else's water in his eye
hurts him with complicity,

his I a house with changing boarders,
painting pictures and plotting murders

his I a wardrobe all bespoke
in alien sizes that bespeak

the formative but foreign babble
that crowds his I as though with scrabble

and squeezes through the mirror
a chatty chimera.

The Boy Who Turned Into a Puppet

*'Civilisation has taught us to renounce cruelty and aggression which once
ran riot in atrocious reality and magical practises . . . In caricature,
however, these forces find a well-guarded playground of their own . . . With
the caricaturist we may relapse into a stratum of the mind where words
and pictures, rules and values lose their well-established meaning, where the
king may be changed into a pear . . . In the eternal child in all of us lie the
true roots of caricature.'*

— GOMBRICH, *Caricature*

My medium makes me think of childhood when I think
Of Mill, the son—as Gombrich says, it makes
The playground erupt into adulthood.
So the adult Mill, in crisis,
Had to go back—reliving like a walker
Yesterday's steps to where he pulled out,
With his handkerchief, the dropped key,

For looking back he saw a face behind his face—
His own, behind his father's: two-way personation.
All his life he'd seen through his father's eyes
Searching for happiness like a perfect
Landscaped garden. But some fairy tales come true
In a trick mirror, where they frighten you.

Look out behind you cry the children's voices—
For he frightened himself, ghosting up behind his back.
The garden imprisoned him; his mask began to rot.
I draw his arms, legs, torso, face. Like me he tried
To draw himself together, and like me he managed
Only a twisted face, a deformation of character—
There, in the trick mirror, his figure jumping.

The Two Heads of Carlyle

His two voices are like rivers—the left
Warm, green and wide, debouching
Into an ocean, but the right a force
Fast, white and cold, and disappearing
Underground. The left voice joins
With earth voices, sky voices, ocean voices—
Hymns, community singing,—
To God and fellow-feeling, reaches out
To flora and fauna, to the people—
Must encompass what it cannot,
In its one-armed embrace: the right arm
Draws back, draws in. The right head listens,
Suffers; adds in brackets guilt,
Need for guidance, shouts the other
Finally down: opposes to that reaching out
The social pyramid, Necessity
Tight as the flight of a braced falcon
Simplifying itself into talons and beak,
Tightening its flight, tightening,
Sharpening itself, narrowing its sights,
Narrowing itself down into its stoop.

Making Myself Scarce

A piece of me is lost
I'm always trying to recover,
Like an unknown woman that I missed:
We would've made such perfect lovers
But she glanced in my compartment as she passed
And chose another;

A feeling in my teens I mislaid
Close to the edge of the council estate,
Beside the turn-off from the main road,
Where the path falters in a flooded rut
Shining dully from a thinning in a cloud—
It's there my right foot

Singularly paces
Feeling above it such a lack of weight,
Lonely outcast from the other pieces,
Haunting the altered council estate,
Where splashed orange in the puddles disperses
Me in the light.

Trying to remember
It's as though the scattered pieces long
For one another, and each member
Trembles for a body, trembles to belong:
A hand on a hill attempting to clamber
With its rubber fingers along

The steep, wet and dimpled paving;
Or my right foot going toe and heel—
Estranged from me, a footloose craving
I look into the hungry night and feel,
Fractured and half-twinned in the double-glazing.
How my hand on the hill

Searches blindly for me—
But expulsions and an early breach,
Or blank in understanding, tore me;
Or I broke where longing made me stretch,
For baulked desires caricature me:
I'm a talking crotch—

Urges I disown—
A foot that haunts a kerb, a hand that gropes;
Pieces with fractious minds of their own,
Like feelings in exile, a lip that creeps
Into a pavement cranny, selves thrown
Like weightless scraps

Unless by force they're drawn
Together—hand and foot and spoken fart,
And I become myself, not helplessly borne
Against my will, but framed by vengeful art—
Till who I am is made from what was torn,
By tearing others apart.

An Irish Joke

The earl smoked at his club,
his premises all ha-ha.
Inside his cloud it said,

'The Irish are niggers
white from eating potatoes.
They're animated picks and spades.
Their island hovers under ours:
a basement, badly lit,
and smelling of wet earth.
They broke the ladders we offered
and carry the rungs around as clubs.'

But Gladstone's not amused.
He feels a sudden heat
at his heels, and sees a floorboard-crack
blink with old newspapers catching fire.

Turkey, Plum Pudding

Diplomatic relations
Crowd the death bed,
So greedy to inherit
Turkey looks trussed up
Under a silver lid.

A frightened eye
Opens in the meat,
Thinking *frog* and kraut
Thinking *roast-beefs*

Thinking after Gillray:
Vulture heads of state
Carve the edible globe—
Such skill they have, the delicate
Long fingers of gourmets!

On velvet cushions, cutlery
Enters in procession.

Turkey hopes the vultures choke
On the hard riches hiding
In the soft plum pudding.

The Dark

Imagining Africa, this strip's
A ladder downward into the dark

Or black roll of film, a negative
That cannot be developed:

The mind that tries to find a way into
Dense forest, vast silence, empty stream

Recoils. Construct a jungle
Out of hothouse details,

Near and far conflated,
Flattened into far—

Find darkness again,
Shadow in intense growth,

Then Rousseau dream clearing, or desert—
Wind wiping the fine sand's memory

Of footsteps, and again darkness.
Take the ladder downward,

Find a frame that's a black window—
Nearness now, not distance

Stops you seeing—something
Pushed up, brushing your lashes:

Near and far conflated,
Flattened into near.

You're back now where you started, square one,
Though the mind that tries to find a way into

Close quarters, near starvation,
Recoils from darkest England:

Lost backstreet tribes; darkness
In the shadow of intense growth.

The Assumption

Gladstone fixes his eyes on the clouds, his ears
On murmurs of a distant sea marked 'Faith'.

Light-headed, his winged collar
Lifts him two inches, then a foot,

But his body is smoke-blackened marble,
His bag is document-heavy,

He tumbles back down.
He tries again, whispering a plea,

Yearning for above and beyond, the blue
Yonder, here a shade of grey.

The High Anglicans are less encumbered
Walking a tightrope between two steeples,

But below them, when they mount higher,
Miles have been reclaimed from the sea

And there are Punch and Judy shows
An iron tower

And further out a pier
Whose reach exceeds its grasp;

The bathers on the beach have telescopes
And watch the shining waves far off,

Paddle in shallow pools
And worship the noise in shells.

The wind blows the clouds on-shore.
A mongrel looks at Gladstone and cocks its leg.

The sky grows overcast
With mute *fumetti*.

Hatred of Gladstone

I've lived with Gladstone half a year.
I talk to him about my class
But it's as though he doesn't hear
Or thinks about them as a mass
Or blur, or sulky beast or sea
Likely to rise against his kind—
They seem subhuman, the enemy
By which we might be undermined.

But then he waxes sympathetic,
Which is worse, thinks up a worker-clone
Or person wholly prosthetic
From bits and pieces of his own,
Displaying his largeness of spirit,
For his heart goes out then to that fiction.
I thicken the gravy then stir it
Silenced by this new conviction

Of understanding, knowing he'll feel
Another mission coming on.
I boil the veg and bin the peel.
He's such a fierce automaton
His breath is steam, his arms are pistons
And what drives him is so inner
It pulls between us such a distance
I dwell on the tastes in my dinner—

All that makes me fully rounded
Slackens my time like detumescence:
All I am is pieces compounded—
Not his hard full single presence
Self-possessed when faced with prostitutes,
Disraeli or Irish angers—
But divergent as my aimless suits
Questioned in the wardrobe by hangers.

A Secret Cyborg

I pecked then hopped, I'd slipped out and blended,
spread my wings and knew I was a sparrow
today as my self extended,
chirping on the handle of a wheelbarrow.

For daily I could feel how I
was more than me, how I ascended
through the veins of the ash into the sky
where all the gaps were mended.

But then my body felt a change
as the thick black thought of the smokestacks
drifted over the hills into my grange
and wafted unseen into my cracks.

There's watts and ohms now in my veins
so part of me dies, this I-morgue
live and wired to others through the mains
becoming a secret cyborg.

My death in life's a cruel sorrow
till I find that I can speed and fly
and plunge into a quick tomorrow,
charged with superpowers I can buy.

Gladstone Speaks from the Afterlife

Hell is other people's memories
Freezing me over
Forever in the same action,

Trapping me in the same frame
Repeated, that contains
Ireland, an axe, a tree

And me, a flat character, the breath
Crushed out of me. I'm shade-thin
In a place that's not a place—

Sun without warmth, flowers without scent,
Music a soundless, head-high
Notation, speech a frozen cloud.

My fingers find
Nothing reciprocal or rough,
Nothing that resists or sticks.

I'm in the landscape where the tunnel starts
And Time the train draws further away
Tightening the frame about me harder and faster.